Friar Bacon

His Discovery of the Miraculous Art of Nature Magic

"The man is insane who writes a secret in any other way than one which will conceal it from the vulgar and make it intelligible only with difficulty - even to scientific men and earnest students"
> - ascribed to Friar Bacon.

The universe is full of magical things, patiently waiting for our wits to grow sharper.
> - Eden Philpotts

A Letter Sent by Friar Roger Bacon to William of Paris Concerning The Secret Operation of Nature and Art and also The Nullity of Magic

Chapter One

Of and against fictitious Appearances and Invocation of Spirits.

That I may carefully render you an answer to your desire, understand, Nature is potent and admirable in her working, yet Art using the advantage of nature as an instrument (experience tells us) is of greater efficacy than any natural activity.

Whatsoever Acts otherwise than by natural or artificial means, is not humane, but merely fictitious and deceitful.

We have many men that by the nimbleness and activity of body, diversification of sounds, exactness of instruments, darkness, or consent, make things seem to be present, which never were really existent in the course of Nature. The world, as any judicious eye may see, groans under such bastard burdens. A Juggler by an handsome sleight of hand, will put a complete lie upon the very sight. The Pythonissæ sometimes speaking from their bellies, otherwhile from the throat, than by the mouth, do create what voices they please, either speaking at hand, or far off, in such a manner, as if a Spirit discoursed with a man, and sometimes as though Beasts bellowed, which is all easily discovered by private laying hollow Canes in the grass, or secret places, for so the voices of men will be known from other creatures.

When inanimate things are violently moved, either in the Morning or Evening twilight, expect no truth therein, but down-right cheating and cousenage.

As for consent, men by it may undertake any thing they please, if so be they have a mutual disposition.

These I mention, as practices wherein neither philosophical Reasons, Art, or power of Nature is prevalent. Beyond these there is a more damnable practice, when men despising the Rules of Philosophy, irrationally call up wicked Spirits, supposing them of Energy to satisfy their desires. In which there is a very vast error, because such persons imagine they have some authority over Spirits, and that Spirits may be compelled by humane authority, which is altogether impossible, since humane Energy or Authority is inferior by much to that of Spirits. Besides, they admit a vaster mistake, supposing such natural instruments, as they use, to be able either to call up, or drive away any wicked Spirit. And they continue their mistake in endeavoring by Invocations, Deprecations or Sacrifices to please Spirits, making them propitious to their design. Without all question, the way is incomparably easier to obtain any thing that is truly good for men, of God, or good

Angels, then of wicked Spirits. As for things which are incommodious for men, wicked Spirits can no further yield assistance, then they have permission, for the sins of the sons of men, from that God, who governs and directs all humane affairs. Hence therefore I shall conclude (these things being beyond, or rather against the Rules of Wisdom) No true Philosopher did ever regard to work by any of these six ways.

Chapter Two

Of Charms, Figures, and their Use.

What men ought to believe touching Figures, Charms, and such stuff, I shall deliver my opinion. Without doubt there is nothing in these days of this kind, but what is either deceitful, dubious, or irrational, which Philosophers formerly invented to hide their secret operations of Nature and Art from the eyes of an unworthy generation. For instance, if the virtue of the Load-stone, whereby it draws iron to it were not discovered, some one or other who hath a mind hereby to cosen the people, so goes about his business, as lest any by-stander should discover the work of attraction to be natural, he calls Figures, and mutters forth some Charms. Thus many things lie dark in Philosophical writings; in which the wiser sort of Readers will express so much discretion, as reject the Figures and Charms, eying the works of Nature and Art, that so they may see the mutual concurrence of animate and inanimate creatures, occasioned by Natures conformity, not any efficacy of Figures or Charms. This is the cause why the unlearned crew have judged such natural or artificial operations to be merely Magical. And some fond Magicians believe that their casting of Figures and Charms was the sole cause of such operations; hereupon leaving their natural and artificial operations have stuck close to their erroneous casting of Figures and Charms. And thus they both have by their own folly deprived themselves of the benefit of the others wisdom. In times past, godly and religious men, or rather God himself, or his good Angels composed several Prayers which yet may retain their primitive virtue. As to this day, in several Countries certain prayers are made over hot irons, and water in the River, &c. By which the innocent are cleared, and guilty condemned; yet all this is done by the Authority of the Church, and her Prelates. Our Priests exercise their holy water, as formerly the Jews did in the Old Testament, in making the water of Trial, whereby the wise was tried, whether she were an adulteress, or honest. Not to instance in others of the like nature. Concerning those Secrets, which are revealed in Magicians writings, although they may contain some truth, yet in regard those very truths are enveloped with such a number of deceits, as it's not very easy to judge betwixt the truth and falsehood, they ought all worthily to be rejected. Neither must men be believed, who would assure us, That Solomon, or some other of our sage Progenitors were Authors of such Books, because those Books are not received either by the Churches Authority, or by any prudent men, but only by a few cheating Companions to be the work of such men. Mine own experience assures me they compose and set forth new works and inventions of their own, in lofty high flown expressions, the more colorably to make their lies pass under the shelter of the Text; prefixing some specious titles, the better to set them off, impudently ascribe such bastard births to famous Authors.

Figures are either composed of words involved in the forms of letters, invented to contain the sense of some speech or prayer; or they are made according to the face of the Heavens in proper and select seasons. The Figures of the former sort must have the same sentence that I gave of prayers formerly; as for Figures and Impressions of the other kind, unless they be made in their peculiar seasons, they are not of any efficacy. And hence it is that all wise men think they affect nothing, who only go according to their prescribed Characters, not at all regarding more than the bare external form. The more knowing sons of Art, dispose all their works of Nature and Art according to the power of the Heavens, casting their work under a right Constellation, no less than the casting it in a right Figure. Now in regard there is much difficulty to discern the motion of Celestial Bodies, many are cousened, and very few know, how to begin their work either profitably or truly. Hence it comes to pass, that the crowd of judicious Mathematicians and Star gazers effect little, and that unprofitable, while the more expert Professors, who sufficiently understand their own Art, attain many conveniences both by their Operations and Judgments in select and proper opportunities: And yet let us take notice, how the Physician, or he that would re-erect a drooping soul, effects his design by the use of Figures or Charms, which in themselves are merely fictitious (as Constantine the Physician is of opinion.) Physicians use Figures or Charms, not for any prevalence in them, but that the raising of the soul is of great efficacy in the curing of the body, and raising it from infirmity to health, by coy and confidence is done by Charms; for they make the Patient receive the Medicine with greater confidence and desire, exciting courage, more liberal belief, hope and pleasure. The Physician then who would magnify his cure, may work some way of exciting hope and confidence in his Patient; not that hereby he should cheat, but stir up the sick to believe he shall recover, which if we pin our faith on Constantine's sleeve, is very tolerable. Upon this account he defends the hanging Charms or Figures about the Neck. The soul no question is of much prevalence by reason of its strong affections over its proper body, as Avicen says in lib. de anima, &c. to which all wise men accord. Hereupon it was, that they concluded sick persons should be delighted by the company of children to play before them, and other pleasing objects. Yea they frequently consent to such things as please the appetite, though they be obnoxious to their disease; because affection, desire and hope of the soul conquers many diseases.

Chapter Three

Sermonis:
Of the force of Speech, and a Check to Magic.

IN regard truth must not receive the least injury, we should take more exact notice how every agent communicates the Virtue and Species which is in it to other extrinsical objects; I mean not only the substantial Virtue, but even Active Accidents, such as are in tertia specie Qualitatis.

As for the Virtues which flows from the Creature, some of them are sensible, some insensible. Man which is both the most noble corporeity, and dignified rational soul, hath no less than other things heat and spirits exhaling from him and so may no less than other things emit and dispose of his Virtues and Species to external Objects.

Some creatures we know have power to metamorphose and alter their objects. As the Basilisk, who kills by sight alone. The Wolf, if she first see a man before the man see him, makes the man hoarse. The Hyæna suffers not the dog which comes within his shadow to bark (as Solinus de mirabili bus mundi, and others) And Aristotle saith, That Female Palm-trees bring forth fruit to maturity by the smell of their Males. And Mares in some Kingdoms impregnate by the smell of Horses (as Solinus affirms.) Aristotle in his Secrets assures us of several other contingencies which issue from the Species and Virtues of Plants and Animals. Hence I argue, If Plants and Animals, which are inferior in dignity to our humane Nature, can emit, then surely may man more abundantly emit Species, Virtues and Colors to the alteration of external Bodies. To this purpose is that, which Aristotle tells us a menstruous woman looking in a glass, infects it with spots, like clouds of blood. Solinus further writes, that in Scythia there are women which have two sights in one eye. (Hence Ovid, Nos et pupilla duplex) and that these women by their glances kill men. And we our selves know, That men of an evil complexion, full of contagious infirmities, as Leprosy, the Falling-sickness, spotted Fever, bleer-eyed, or the like, infects those men in their company: While on the other side, men of a sound and wholesome complexion, especially young men, do by their very presence exhilarate and comfort others; which no question, as Galen in his Techne, proceeds from their pure spirits wholesome and delightsome vapors, their sweet natural color, and from such Species and Virtues as they emit.

That man whose soul is defiled with many heinous sins, his Body infirm, his Complexion evil, and hath a vehement fancy and desire to hurt his neighbor, may bring more inconveniences, then another man. The Reason may be, the Nature of Complexion and infirmity yields obedience to the thoughts of the Heart, and is more augmented by the intervention of our desires. Hence it is that a leprous person, who is solicitous, desirous and fancying to infect some one or other in the room, may more easily and forcibly effect it, than he which hath no such intention, fancy or desire. For (as Avicen observes in the fore cited place) the nature of the body is obedient to the thoughts, and more intent fancies of the soul. And (as Avicen in the 3dMetaph. affirms) the thought is the first mover, after that the desire is made conformable to the thought, then after that the natural virtue, which is in the members, obeys the desire and thought; and thus it is both in good and bad effects. Hence it is that a young man of a good Complexion, healthful, fair, well featured Body, having his soul not debauched with sin, but of a strong fancy and vehement desire to compass the effecting of some magnificent design, withal adding the power of his Virtues, Species and natural heat; He may by the force of these Spirits, Vapors and influences work both more powerfully and vehemently, than if he should want any of these fore going qualifications, especially strong affections and forcible imaginations. Hence I conclude, Men by the concurrence of the foresaid Causes, Words and Works being the Instruments, bring great undertakings to perfection.

As for words, they are hatched within, by the thoughts and desires of the mind, sent abroad by heat, Vocal arteries, and motion of the Spirits. The places of their generation are in open passages, by which there is a great efflux of such spirits, heat, vapors, virtues, and Species, as are made by the soul and heart. And therefore words may so far cause alterations by these parts or passages, as their Nature will extend. For it's evident, that breathings, yawnings, several resolutions of Spirits and heat come through these open passages from the heart and inward parts: Now if these words come from an infirm and evil complexionated body, they are constantly obnoxious. But if from a pure sound and wholesome constitution, they are very beneficial and comfortable. It's clear then, That the bare generation and prolation of words joined with desire and intention are considerable in natural operations. Hereupon we do justly say, Vox viva magnum habet virtutem; Living words are of great Virtue. Not that they have any such Virtue of doing or undoing, as Magicians speak of, but only they have the Virtue of Nature, which makes me put in this Caution of being extream cautelous herein. For a man may, as many have already done, err on both hands: Some wholly denying any operation of words: Others superfluously decline to a Magical use thereof. Our duties should be to have a care of such Books, as are fraught with Charms, Figures, Orizons, Conjurations, Sacrifices, or the like, because they are purely Magical. For instance, the Book De Officiis Spirituum, liber de morte animæ, liber de arte notoria with infinite others, containing neither precepts of Nature or Art, having nothing save Magical Fopperies. Yet here withal we must remember, there are many Books commonly reputed to be Magical, but have no other fault then discovering the dignity of wisdom. What Books are suspicious, and what not; every discreet Readers experience will show him. The Book which discovers natural or artificial operations embrace; that which is void of either or leave both, as suspicious and unworthy the consideration of any wise man. 'Tis usual with Magicians, to treat of both unnecessary and superfluous subjects. 'Twas excellently said of Isaac (in lib. de Febribus,) The rational soul is not impeded in its operations, unless by the Manacles of ignorance. And Aristotle is of opinion, (in lib. secret.) That a clear and strong intellect, being impregnated by the influences of divine Virtue, may attain to anything which is necessary. And in 3d Meteor, he says, There is no influence or power, but from God. In the Conclusion of his Ethics, There is no Virtue, whether Moral or Natural without divine influence. Hence it is, that when we discourse of particular agents, we exclude not the Regiment of the universal Agent, and first Cause of all things. For every first Cause hath more influence on the Effect, than any second Cause, as he speaks in the first proposition of Causes.

Chapter Four

Of Admirable Artificial Instruments.

That I may the better demonstrate the inferiority and indignity of Magical power to that of Nature or Art, I shall a while discourse on such admirable operations of Art and Nature, as have not the least Magic in them, afterwards assign them their Causes and Frames. And first of such Engines, as are purely artificial.

It's possible to make Engines to sail withal, as that either fresh or salt water vessels may be guided by the help of one man, and made sail with a greater swiftness, than others will which are full of men to help them.

It's possible to make a Chariot move with an inestimable swiftness (such as the Currus falcati were, wherein our fore fathers of old fought,) and this motion to be without the help of any living creature.

It's possible to make Engines for flying, a man sitting in the midst whereof, by turning only about an Instrument, which moves artificial Wings made to beat the Air, much after the fashion of a Birds flight.

It's possible to invent an Engine of a little bulk, yet of great efficacy, either to the depressing or elevation of the very greatest weight, which would be of much consequence in several Accidents: For hereby a man may either ascend or descend any walls, delivering himself or comrads from prison; and this Engine is only three fingers high, and four broad.

A man may easily make an Instrument, whereby one man may in despite of all opposition, draw a thousand men to himself, or any other thing, which is tractable.

A man may make an Engine, whereby without any corporal danger, he may walk in the bottom of the Sea, or other water. These Alexander (as the Heathen Astronomer assures us) used to see the secrets of the deeps.

Such Engines as these were of old, and are made even in our days. These all of them (excepting only that instrument of flying, which I never saw or know any who hath seen it, though I am exceedingly acquainted with a very prudent man, who hath invented the whole Artifice) with infinite such like inventions, Engines and devices are feasible, as making of Bridges over Rivers without pillars or supporters.

Chapter Five

Of Perspective Artificial Experiments.

The physical figuration of rays are found out to be very admirable. Glasses and Perspectives may be framed, to make one thing appear many, one man an Army, the Sun and Moon to be as many as we please. As Pliny in the 2d Book, Nat. Hist. chap. 30. saith, That Nature so disposes of vapors, as two Suns, and two Moons ; yea sometimes three Suns shine together in the Air. And by the same Reason one thing may in appearance be multiplied to an infinity, in regard that after any creature hath exceeded his own virtue (as Aristotle cap. de vacuo.) no certain bounds is to be assigned it.

This design may seem advantageous to strike terrors into an Enemies Camp or Garrison, there being a multiplication of appearances of Stars, or men assembled purposely to destroy them; Especially if the following design be conjoined to the former (viz.) Glasses so cast, that things at hand may appear at distance, and things at distance, as hard at hand: yea so far may the design be driven, as the least letters may be read, and things reckoned at an incredible distance, yea stars shine in what place you please. A way, as is verily believed, Julius Cæsar took by great Glasses from the Coasts of France, to view the site and disposition of both the Castles and SeaTowns in great Britain. By the framing of Glasses, bodies of the largest bulk, may in appearance be contracted to a minute volume, things little in themselves show great, while others tall and lofty appear low and creeping, things creeping and low, high and mighty, things private and hidden to be clear and manifest. For as Socrates did discover a Dragon, whose pestiferous breathings and influences corrupted both City and Country thereabouts, to have his residence in the Caverns of the Mountains. So may any other thing done in an Enemies Camp or Garrison, be discovered. Glasses may be framed to send forth Species, and poisonous infectious influences, whither a man pleases. And this invention Aristotle showed Alexander, by which he erecting the poison of a Basilisk upon the Wall of a City, which held out against his Army, conveyed the very poison into the City it self. Glasses may be so framed and placed, as that any man coming into a room, shall undoubtedly imagine he sees heaps of gold, silver, precious stones, or what you please, though upon his approach to the place he shall perceive his mistake.

It's then folly to seek the effecting that by Magical Illusions, which the power of Philosophy can demonstrate.

To speak of the more sublimate powers of Figurations, leading and congregating rays by several Fractions and reflections to what distance we please, so as any object may prove combustible. It's evident by Perspectives they burn backward and forward, which Authors have treated on in their Books. That which is the most strange of Figurations and Mouldings, is the description of

Celestial Bodies, both according to their Longitude and Latitude, in such Corporeal Figures, as they naturally move by their diurnal motion. An Invention of more satisfaction to a discreet head, than a Kings Crown.

But this will suffice as to Figurations, though we might produce infinite prodigies of the like Nature.

Chapter Six

Concerning strange Experiments.

To our former discourse we may adjoin such work as are effected without Figurations. We may have an artificial composition of Saltpeter, and other ingredients; or of the oil of Red Petrolei, and other things, or with Maltha, Naphtha, with such like, which will burn at what distance we please, with which Pliny reports, Lib. 2. Chap. 104. that he kept a City against the whole Roman Army: For by casting down Maltha he could burn a Soldier, though he had on his Armor. In the next place, to these we may place the Grecian fire, and other combustibles. To proceed, Lamps may be made to burn, and waters to keep hot perpetually. For I know many things which are not consumed in the fire, as the Salamanders skin Talk, with others, which by some adjunct both are inflamed and shine, yet are not consumed, but rather purified. Besides these, we may speak of diverse admirable pieces of Nature. As the making Thunder and Lighting in the Air; yea with a greater advantage of horror, then those which are only produced by Nature. For a very competent quantity of matter rightly prepared (the bigness of ones thumb) will make a most hideous noise and coruscation, this may be done several ways; by which a City or Army may be overcome, much after the fashion as Gideon overcame that vast Army of the Midianites with three hundred men, by the breaking of their Pitchers, and shining of their Lamps, together with the sudden leaping forth of the fire, and inestimable crackings. These would appear strange, if they were designed to their just height both of proportion and matter. I might produce many strange works of another kind, which though they bring no sensible profit, yet contain an ineffable spectacle of wit, and may be applied to the probation of all such secrets, as the ignorant crew will not embrace. Such might I name the attraction, of Iron to the Loadstone, a thing so incredulous, as none save an eye-witness would believe. And in this attraction of Iron, experience will show a diligent searcher, more wonders than any vulgar capacity can entertain.

But to proceed to greater, and more than these. There is an attraction of gold, silver, and all other metals, by a certain stone, much after the same manner. Besides one stone will run to the heap. Plants may have their mutual concurrence, and the parts of sensible creatures locally divided, will naturally move to a mutual embracement. The consideration whereof makes me think, that there is not any thing, whether in divine or outward matters too difficult for my faith. To proceed higher, the whole power of the Mathematics may compose a spherical Engine, according to Ptolemy's frame in eight Almagest; which sincerely describes both longitude and latitude of all Celestial Bodies; but to give them a natural diurnal motion is not in the power of the Mathematics. However a discreet head-piece would do well to try the making hereof of such materials and artifice, as it might have a natural diurnal motion. Which seems to me possible; and because many things are moved with the motion of the Heavens, as Comets, the Sea tides, with several other things, which are turned about either in the whole or in part. Such a work might be thought more miraculous, and of a vaster benefit than any thing hitherto mentioned. For the perfecting of this would frustrate all other, whether the more curious, or the more vulgar Astronomical Instruments, which surely would be more valuable than a Kings Coffers; and yet there may matters be brought to pass, which though they will not reach so near a miracle, yet of far greater public and private profit. As the producing so much gold or silver, as we please, not by the work of Nature yet accomplishment of Art: seeing there may be ten and seven ways of gold, eight by the mixture of silver with gold; and the first way is made by sixteen parts of gold with some parts of silver, which will attain the four and twentieth degree of gold, al- ways augmenting one degree of gold with one of silver, and so for the mixture of brass with gold. So the last way is by the four and twenty degrees of pure gold without mixture of other metal. And beyond this, Nature knows no further progress, as experience tells us. Though Art may augment gold in the degrees of purity, even to infiniteness, and complete silver, without the least cheat: And yet that which seems more rare than all this is, That though the rational soul (hath so far its free-will, as) it cannot be compelled, yet may effectually be excited, induced and disposed freely to alter its affections, desires and behaviors to the dictates of another man. And this may not only be practiced upon one particular person, but upon a whole Army, City, or

Body of a Nation living under one Region, if we believe experience. And this experience, Aristotle disclosed in his Book of Secrets, both of an Army, Region and single person. And thus I have well nigh finished my thoughts of Nature and Art.

Chapter Seven

Of Retarding the Accidents of Old age, and Prolongation of Life.

The furthest attainment, which the complement of Art, joined with the whole Energy of Nature can reach unto, is the Prolongation of Life to a very old date. How far this is attainable, manifold experience hath showed us. Pliny reports, That Pollio, a man of a strong body and mind, lived much longer then men usually now: of whom Octavius Augustus enquiring, what course he took to live so long? was answered ænigmatically, he used Oil without, and Mulsum within (now according to the opinion of some, it's eight parts of water, and nine of honey) I might produce many examples of the same quality: as that which fell out in the days of King William; A Countryman plowing in the field, found a golden vessel, containing a certain liquor, which he supposing to be the Dew of Heaven, washed his face withal, and drunk of it, whereby he became renewed in spirit, body and excellency, De bubulio factus est Bajulus Regis Sicilie, from a Plow-man he was made Porter to the King of Sicily. And the Popes Letters assures us, That Almannus, held Prisoner by the Saracens, through the use of a Medicine lived five hundred years. For the King, whose Captive he was, having received this Medicine from the Ambassadors of the great King, and being suspicious of them, made trial hereof upon this Captive, which was brought him for that purpose. And the Lady of the Woods in great

Britanny searching for a white Hind, found an Ointment, wherewith the Keeper of the Woods anointed his whole body, except the soles of his feet, and he lived three hundred years without any corruption, save in the soles of his feet, which had some passions. We our selves know it frequent in these days, that plain Country men, without the advantage so much as of a Physicians advice, live very healthfully an hundred years, or little less. And these are the rather confirmed by the operations of Animals, as Harts, Eagles, Serpents, and many other, who by the efficacy of heart or stones, have renewed their youth: And wise men seeing that even bruits could reach so far to their Prolongation, adjudging it no less feasible by reasonable men, set themselves on the Spurre to find out this secret. Hereupon Artefius from his own ingenuity, having found the Secrets, of Stones, Herbs, Sensibles, &c. both for the knowledge of Nature, and especially the Prolongation of Life, did rejoice, that he had lived 1025 years. Further, to confirm this Assertion of the Prolongation of Life, it's considerable, That man naturally is immortal, that is to say, Potens non mori, hath a possibility of not dying. Yea, even after his fall, he might live a thousand years, though by degrees the length of life was abbreviated. Hence it follows, that this abbreviation is Accidental, and consequentially may be repaired in whole or in part; and upon search we shall find the accidental cause of this corruption, is not from the Heavens, or any other than the defect of true Government of our health. In that our Fathers are corrupt and imbeciles, they beget sons of a corrupt complexion and composition, and their children upon the same score are corrupted. Thus the Pedigree of corruption is deprived from Fathers to sons, until we settle upon our heirs an assured abbreviation of our days. Yet this doth not conclude, That to perpetuity there shall succeed an abbreviation of our life, since there is a positive period set to our life, men may live till they be eighty years, though then their days be but labor and sorrow.

Now if every man would from the breast exercise a complete Regiment of health (which consists in such things as have relation to Meat, Drink, Sleep, Waking, Motion, Rest, Evacuation, Retention, Air, and the Passions of the mind) He might find a remedy resisting his proper malady. For upon the prosecution of such a Regiment, one might arrive at the uttermost limit of that Nature he had from his Parents will permit, and be led to the very last period of Nature beyond which there is no further progress; because it doth little or nothing avail against the corruption of our Ancestors: and yet the great impossibility of any mans so ordering himself in a mean, in all the fore-mentioned things, as the Regiment of health exacts, wherefore abbreviation of our days does not only from our Progenitors, but hath its advantages from the want of Regiment. However the Art of Physick sufficiently determines this. Although nor rich, or poor, wise or ignorant, no nor the most accurate Physicians themselves, do accomplish this Regiment in themselves or others, as every eye can discern; Yet Nature is not deficient in Necessaries, or

Art any ways incomplete, but rather is advantageous to make insurrections and irruptions against, and so far into these accidental passions, as they are either wholly or in part rooted out. At first, and in the beginning of our ages declining, the remedy was easy: But since we have five thousand years or more disadvantage, the Cure is more craggy.

But waving the Inconveniences wise men moved by the considerations forementioned, have endeavored to find out the means and ways, which not only are forcible against the defects of every mans proper Regiment, but also against the corruptions of our Parents: Not that hereby they can attain to the years of Adam or Artesius, by reason of the growing corruption, but that our days may be augmented an hundred years, or more, above the ordinary age of most men in these days. And though it be impossible absolutely to retard the accidents of old age, yet hereby they may mitigate them, so as life will happily be prorogued beyond the common account, yet always within the ultimate circuit of Nature. There is a bounder of Nature, set in men since their Fall. There is a bounder of every particulate man arising from the proper corruption of his Parents. Beyond both these bounders it's impossible to pass; yet happily one may arrive beyond the latter: nor yet so far to go beyond it, as that the wisest of men can never reach the former. Although there be a possibility and aptitude of Nature to proceed to that boundary our first Parents set them. Let no man think this strange, since this aptitude extends itself to immortality, as appears both before the fall, and shall be evident after the Resurrection.

Perhaps you may object, that neither Aristotle, Plato, Hippocrates, or Galen ever attained that prolongation. I shall answer, They have not attained the knowledge of many ordinary truths, which other ingenious heads have found out; and if so, they may easily miscarry in a business of such weighty consequence, though they made it their study: especially, if we consider, how they were burdened with other impertinencies, and so were sooner brought to their gray hairs, spending the inch of their Candles in more debased and vulgar subjects, than in finding out the ways to so great Secrets. We are not ignorant Aristotle says in his Predicaments, That the Quadrature of a Circle is possible, yet not then known, Yea he confesses, himself and all his Predecessors were ignorant hereof, yet we in our times know it. Now if Aristotle did come short in such a trivial, much more might he in the deep mysteries of Nature. Even in these days wise men are ignorant of many things, which the most ordinary capacity shall understand ere long. Thus the Objection is of little force.

Chapter Eight

Of obscuring the Mysteries of Art and Nature.

After an enumeration of some few examples concerning the prevalence of Nature and Art (that by these few we may gather many,) by these parts the whole; and so from particulars, universals, which will demonstrate the unnecessary aspiring to Magic, since both Nature and Art afford such sufficiency. I shall now endeavors a methodical procedure in singulars, laying open both the causes and ways in particular: and yet I will call to mind how as Secrets are not committed to Goats-skins and Sheeps-pelts, that every clown may understand them, if we follow Socrates or Aristotle. For the latter in his Secreta Secretarum affirmes, He breaks the Heavenly Seal, who communicates the Secrets of Nature and Art; the disclosing of Secrets and Mysteries, producing many inconveniences. In this case Aulus Gellius in Noct. Atti. de Collatione Sapientum, says, It's but folly to proffer Lettuce to an Ass, since he's content With his Thistles. Et in lib. lapidum, The divulging of Mysteries is the diminution of their Majesty, nor indeed continues that to be a Secret, of which the whole fry of men is conscious.

For that which all men, which wise, and the more noted men affirm is truth. That therefore which is held by the multitude, as a multitude, must be false; I mean of that multitude, which is distinct from knowing men. The multitude, it's true, agree with wise men in the more vulgar conceptions of their mind; but when they ascend to the proper principles and conclusions of Sciences and Arts, they much dissent (striving to get only the appearances in Sophisms and subtleties which wise men altogether reject.) And this their ignorance of the properties and Secrets, makes the division from knowing men. Though the common conception of the mind, have all one Rule and Agreement with knowing men. Yet as for common things, they are of small value, nor enquirable for themselves, but rather for particular and proper ends.

The Reason then, why wise men have obscured their Mysteries from the multitude, was, because of their deriding and flighting wise mens Secrets of wisdom, being also ignorant to make a right use of such excellent matters. For if an accident help them to the knowledge of a worthy Mystery, they wrest and abuse it to the manifold inconvenience of persons and communities. He's then not discreet, who writes and Secrets, unless he conceal it from the vulgar, and make the more intelligent pay some labor and sweat before they understand it. In this stream the whole fleet of wise men have failed from the beginning of all, obscuring many ways the obtuse parts of wisdom from the capacity of the generality. Some by Characters and Verses have delivered many Secrets. Others by ænigmatical and figurative words, as Aristotle says, (in lib. Secret, O Alexander, I shall disclose to you the greatest of Secrets, which it becomes you by divine Assistance to keep secret, and perfect the thing proposed. Take then the Stone, which is no Stone, which is in every man, and in every place, and in all times; and it shall be called the Philosophers Egg, and the Terminus Ovi. And thus we find multitudes of things obscured in the Writings and Sciences of men, which no man without his Teacher can unveil.

Thirdly, they have obscured their Secrets by their manner of writing, as by Consonants without Vowels, none knowing how to read them, unless he know the signification of those words. Thus the Hebrews, Caldees, Arabians, nay the major part of men do most an end write their Secrets, which causes a great obscurity amongst them, especially amongst the Hebrews. For as Aristotle says in his fore recited Book, God gave them all manner of Wisdom long before they were Philosophers: And all Nations had their Originals of Philosophy from the Hebrews, as Albumazar in lib. Introductorii Majoris; and other Philoso phers, with Josephus lib.I. & lib.8. Antiquit. makes it evident.

Fourthly, this obscuring is occasioned by the mixture of several sorts of Letters, for so the Ethnic Astronomer hid his knowledge, writing it in Hebrew, Greek and Latin Letters altogether.

Fifthly, This obscuring was by their inventing other letters, then those which were in use in their own, or any other Nation, being framed merely by the pattern of their own fancy, which surely is the greatest impediment; yet this was the practice of Artesius in lib. de Secretis Naturæ.

Sixthly, they used not the Characters of Letters, but other Geometrical Characters, which have the power of Letters according to the several Position of Points, and Markes. And these he likewise made use of.

Seventhly, there is a greater Art of obscuring, which is called Ars Notoria, which is the Art of Noting and Writing, with what brevity, and in what manner we desire. This way the Latins have delivered many things. I held it necessary to touch at these obscurings, because it may fall out, I shall throw the magnitude of our Secrets discourse this way, that I may help you so far as I may.

How to make the Philosophers Egg

Chapter Nine

In aliis Adverg.

Of the Manner to make the Philosophers Egg

Now I shall methodically handle those things I promised above, the dissolving the Philosophers Egg, and finding out the parts thereof; a work which will give beginning to other enterprises. Make a diligent purification of the Calx with the waters of the Alkali, and other acute waters, grind it by several contrition with the salts, and burn it with many assations, that the earth may be perfectly separated from other elements, which I hold worthy the longitude of my stature. Understand it if you can. For without doubt there will be a composition of Elements, and so it will be part of that Stone which is no Stone, which is in every man, and in every place of man; and you may find this this in all the seasons of the year in its place. Then take oyl after the form of a Saffron-cheese, and so viscouous first (as not to be smitten asunder by a stroke) divide the whole fiery virtue, and separate it by dissolution, and let it be dissolved in acute water, of a temperate acuteness, with a slight fire, and let it be boiled till his fatness, as the fatness of flesh be separated by distillation, that nothing of the unctuousness may issue forth; and let this fiery virtue be distilled in the water of Urine. Afterwards boil it in Vinegar, until the least part, which is the cause of adduction be dried up, and the fiery virtue may be had; but if there be no regard of it, again let it be made. Mind and search what I say: for the speech is difficult. The Oil is dissolved in acute waters, or in common Oil which works more expressly, or in acute Oil of Almonds upon the fire; so as the Oil be separated, and the spirit remain occult, in the parts of living creatures, Sulphur and Arsenic. For the stones, in which the Oil of humidity overflows, have their terminus in the union of its parts: for there is no vehement union, but one may be dissolved from another by the nature of water, which is the subject of liquefaction in the spirit, which is the Medium betwixt the dry parts and the Oil. The dissolution being made there will remain in the spirit, a pure humidity, vehemently mixed with dry parts, which are moved in it, when the fire resolves it, which is sometimes called of the Philosophers, Sulphur fusible, sometimes Oil, other while an airy humor, sometime a conjunctive substance, which the fire separates not, sometimes Camphor: and if you please, this is the Philosophers Egg, or rather the Terminus and end of the Egg; and it came to us from these Oils, and may be esteemed amongst the subtleties, when it is purged and separated from the water and oil in which it is. Further, the Oil is corrupted by grinding it with defecating things, as with salt or Atrimentum, and by assation, because there is a passion arising from the contrary; and afterwards it is to be sublimated, until it be deprived of its oleagineity, and because its as Sulphur or Arsenic amongst Minerals, it may be prepared, even as it is. Yet it's better to boil it in waters that are temperate in acuity, until it be purged and whitened. Which wholesome exaltation is made either in hot or moist fire: The distillation must be re-iterated, that it may sufficiently receive its goodness, until it be rectified, the signs of its last rectification are candor and crystalline serenity: And when other things grow black, by fire, this grows white, is cleansed, shines with clearness and admirable splendor. From this water and its earth comes Argentum vivum in Minerals, and when the matter hath waxed white, this way it is congealed; the Stone of Aristotle, which is no Stone, it's set in a Pyramid a hot place, or (if you please) in the belly of an Horse or Ox, and it imitates an acute Fever. For from seven to fourteen, and from that it sometimes proceeds to one and twenty, that the Feces of the Elements may be dissolved in its water, before it be separate: The dissolution and distillation is to be iterated, until it be rectified. And here is the end of this intention. Yet know that when you have consummated your work, you are then to begin.

Another Secret I shall show you, you must prepare Argentum vivum by mortifying it with the vapor of Tin for Pearls, and with the vapor of Lead for the Stone Iberus; then let it be ground with desiccating things, and Attramentis, and the like, as is said, and let there be an assation: Then let there be a sublimation if for Pearls twelve times; if for redness one and twenty times, until the humidity within it be totally corrupted. Nor is it possible, that its humidity be separated by vapor, as the fore-said oil; because its vehemently mixed with its dry parts; nor doth it constitute, as in the foresaid metals. In this Chapter you may be deceived, unless you distinguish of the signification of the words. It's now high time I involve the third Chapter: that you acquire the Calx, the Calx of the body, which you intend, the body is calcined, when it is appodiated, i.e. that the humor in it may be corrupted by salt, and with salt Armoniack and vinegar, and sometimes with burning things, and with Sulphur and Arsenic: and sometimes bodies are fed with Argentum vivum, and sublimated from them, until they remain putrid. The claves of the Art are congelation, resolution, inceration, proportion; and another way purification, distillation, separation, calcination and fixation, and then you may acquiesce.

Chapter Ten

Of the same Subject another way

IN the Arabian year, you entreated me for some Secrets. Take then the Stone, and calcine it with a light assation and strong contrition, or with acute things. But in the end mingle it a little with sweet water, and compound a Laxative Medicine of seven things (if you will) or of six, or of five, or as many as you please; but my mind rests in two things, whose proportion is better than the other fixed proportion, or thereabouts, as experience will teach you. Resolve notwithstanding the gold at the fire, and tried it better; but if you will credit me, take one thing that is the Secret of Secrets of Nature, able to do Miracles. Let it be mixed from two or more, or a Phoenix, which is a singular creature at the fire, and incorporate by a strong motion: to which if hot liquor four or five times be applied, you have the composition. Yet afterwards the coelestial nature is deliberated, if you infuse hot water three or four times. Divide therefore the week from the strong in several vessels, if you believe me: Let that which is good be evacuated. Again, use the powder, and the water which remains, carefully express: For of a certain, it will produce the parts of the powder, not incorporated: therefore take the water by it self; because the powder exiccated from it has power to be incorporated into the Laxative Medicine. Work therefore as formerly, until you distinguish the strong from the weak, and apply the powder three, four, five times or oftener, and work always the way: And if you cannot work with hot waters, do it with water of Alkali, and by such acute things you make the violence of the Medicine. But if by reason of the acuity and softness of the Medicine it be broken, the powder, being applied, apply very carefully more of the hard and soft. But if it be by reason of the abundance of the powder apply more of the Medicine; if it be by reason of the strength of the water, water it with pistils; and congregate the matter, as you can, and separate the water by little and little, and it will return to its state, which water you must exsiccate: for it contains both powder and water of the Medicine, which are to be incorporated, as the principle powder. Here you may not sleep, because here is contained a very great and profitable Secret. If you rightly order in a right series of things, the parts of the Shrub or Willow, they will keep natural union: and do not deliver this to oblivion, for it is profitable for many things. You must mingle Pearls with the made union: as I think there will arise some thing like the Stone Iberus: and without doubt it mortifies that which is to be mortified by the vapor of Lead. You shall find Lead, if you express the living from the dead; and the dead you must bury in Olibanum and Sarcocolla. Keep this Secret, for it is of some profit, and so must you do with the vapor of Pearls, and the Stone Tagus, and you must (as I have said) bury the dead.

Chapter Eleven

Of the same Subject another way.

TO your desire in the Arabian year, I return this Answer. You must have the Medicine which may be dissolved in the thing liquefied and steeped in it, and penetrate its interior parts, and may be mingled with it; and it may not be a fugitive servant, but transmute it. Let it be mingled by reason of the spirit, and let it be fixed by the Calx of the metal; it is to be thought that fixion is prepared, when the body and spirit are set in its place, and the spirit is made a body. Take then of the bones of Adam, and of the Calx the same weight; let there be six to the Stone Tagi, and five to the stone of Pearl; let them be ground with Aqua vitae, whose property it is to dissolve all other things, so as in it they are dissolved and assated, until it be incerate, id est, let the parts be united, as the parts in wax. The sign of inceration is, that the Medicine liquefies upon iron very hot. Then let it be put in the same water in some hot and moist place, or let it hang in the vapor of waters made very hot: after that dissolve and congeal them against the Sun, Afterwards take Saltpeter, and argentum vivum shall be converted into lead : And again, wash the lead with it, and mundifie it, that it may be the next to silver, and then work as a pious man, and also the whole weight must be 30. But yet of Saltpeter L U R UV O P O Vir Can Utriet Sulphuris : and so you may make Thunder and Lightning, if you understand the Artifice : but you must observe, whether I speak ænigmatically, or according to the truth. Some men have supposed otherwise: For it is told me that you must resolve all into its first matter, of which you have Aristotle speaking in vulgar and known places, which makes me silent herein. When you have this, you have pure, simple and equal Elements. And this you may do by contrary thing and various operations, which formerly I have called the Claves of the Art. And Aristotle says, that the equality of potencies excludes action, and passion, and corruption. And these things Averrho's affirms, reproving Galen. And this Medicine is esteemed the more pure and simple which may be found, which is prevalent against Fevers, passions of the mind and body. Farewell. Whoever unlocks these, hath a key which opens and no man shuts: and when he hath shut no man opens.

Finis

www.ingramcontent.com/pod-product-compliance
Lightning Source LLC
Chambersburg PA
CBHW071752090426
42738CB00011B/2656